A Children's Picture Coloring Book

For The Children's Picture-Word & Simple Sentence Book

By

Dr. Harry R. Irving, Ed. D.

Illustrations By Graphics Factory

Fully Reproducible

Primary Grades & ESOL Students

Order this book online at www.trafford.com
or email orders@trafford.com

Most Trafford titles are also available at major online book retailers.

Note for Librarians: A cataloguing record for this book is available from Library
and Archives Canada at www.collectionscanada.ca/amicus/index-e.html

Printed in Victoria, BC, Canada.

ISBN: 978-1-4269-0655-8 (Soft)
ISBN: 978-1-4269-0657-2 (e-book)

*Our mission is to efficiently provide the world's finest, most comprehensive book publishing
service, enabling every author to experience success. To find out how to publish your book, your
way, and have it available worldwide, visit us online at www.trafford.com*

Trafford rev. 11/04/2009

www.trafford.com

North America & international
toll-free: 1 888 232 4444 (USA & Canada)
phone: 250 383 6864 ♦ fax: 812 355 4082

Table of Contents

Introduction

Purpose

The book is designed to assist parents and teachers in developing Children's Language Arts Skills, at home and at the school primary grade levels.

Description

This "Children's Picture Coloring Book", consisting of 180 pictures of some animals and common things , that children will enjoy coloring, is designed to accompany the author's basic book, "A Children's Picture-Word and Simple Sentence Book".

Supplements

In addition to this coloring book and his basic book, the author has developed three assessment tools,   (1) an eighteen Word search and eighteen Crossword puzzles sheets book, (2) an eighteen Picture-word quizzes sheets book, and (3) a 180 Flip charts and Name tags Packet" also, to accompany his basic book and for the purposes of measuring what the child has learned.

Further, below is a list of the author's works that are a must and parents, teachers, and students are encouraged to purchase them. Each sold separately.

1) **"A Children's Picture-Word and Simple Sentence Book"**
2) **"Picture Coloring Book"**
3) **"Word Search and Crossword Puzzles Book"**,
4) **"Picture-Word Quizzes Book"**
5) **"Flip Charts and Name Tags Packet"**

Reproducible

The author grants teachers permission to photocopy the pages from this book for classroom use.

Name_____

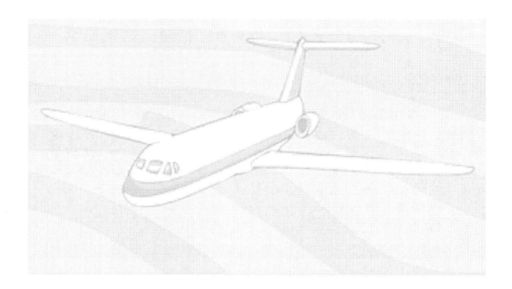

_____

_____

_____

_____

Name_____

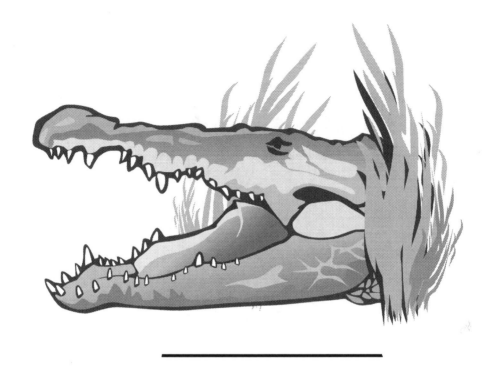

_____

_____

_____

_____

Name_____

_____

_____

_____

_____

Name_____

_____

_____

_____

_____

Name_____

_____

_____
_____
_____

Name_____

_____

_____

_____

_____

Name_____

_____

_____

_____

_____

Name_____

—————————————

_____

_____

_____

Name_____

_____

_____

_____

_____

Name_____

_____

_____

_____

_____

Name_____

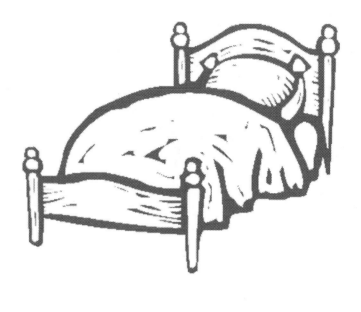

_____

_____

_____

_____

Name_____

_____

_____

_____

_____

Name_____

_____

_____

_____

_____

Name_____

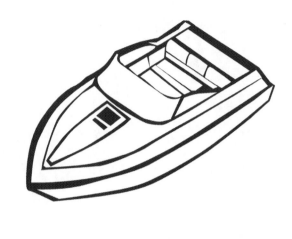

_____

_____

_____

_____

Name_____

_____

_____
_____
_____

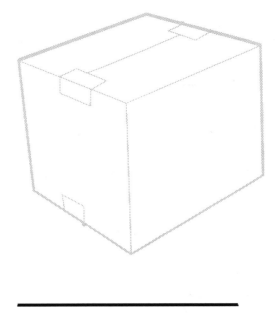

_____

_____

_____

_____

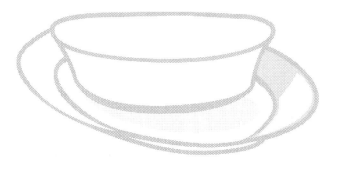

_____

_____

_____

_____

Name_____

_____

_____
_____

_____

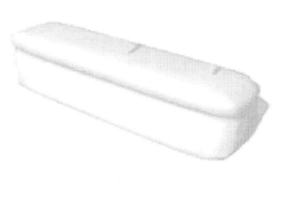

_____

_____

_____

_____

Name_____

_____

_____

_____

_____

Name_____

_____

_____

_____

_____

Name_____

_____

_____

_____

_____

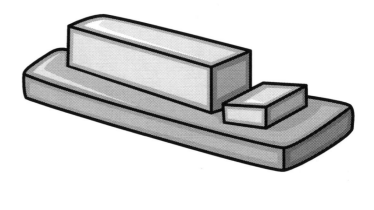

_____

_____

_____

_____

Name_____

_____

_____

_____

_____

24

Name_____

_____

_____

_____

_____

Name_____

_____

_____

_____

_____

_____

_____

_____

_____

Name_____

_____

_____

_____

_____

Name_____

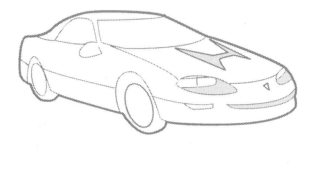

_____

_____

_____

_____

Name_____

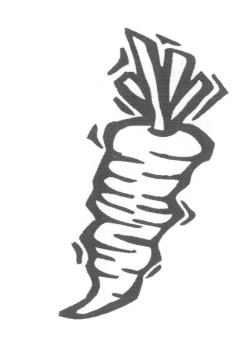

_____

_____

_____

_____

Name_____

_____

_____

_____

_____

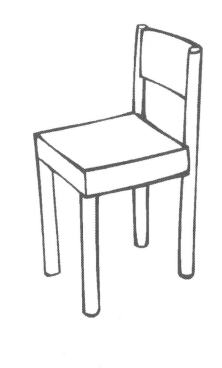

_____

_____

_____

_____

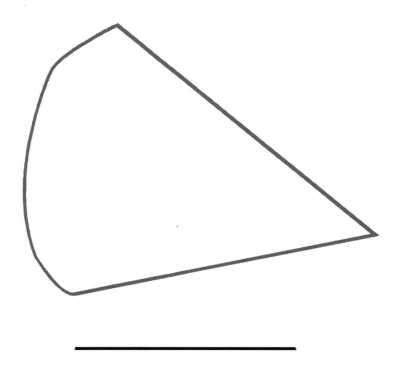

_____

_____
_____
_____

Name_____

_____

_____

_____

_____

Name_____

_____

_____

_____

_____

35

Name_____

_____

_____

_____

_____

Name_____

_____

_____

_____

_____

_____

_____

_____

_____

Name_____

_____

_____
_____
_____

Name_____

_____

_____

_____

_____

_____

_____

_____

_____

Name_____

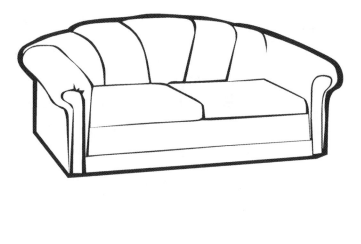

_____

_____

_____

_____

Name_____

_____

_____

_____

_____

Name_____

_____

_____

_____

_____

_____

Name_____

_____

_____

_____

_____

Name_____

_____

_____
_____
_____

_____

_____
_____
_____

Name_____

_____

_____

_____

_____

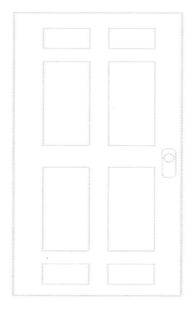

_____

_____

_____

_____

_____

_____

_____

_____

Name_____

_____

_____

_____

_____

Name_____

_____

_____

_____

_____

Name_____

_____

_____

_____

_____

Name_____

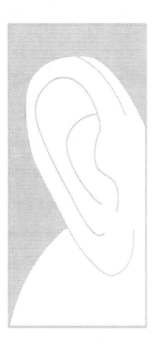

_____

_____

_____

_____

Name_____

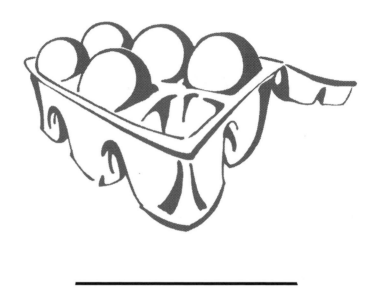

_____

_____

_____

_____

_____

_____

_____

_____

Name_____

_____

_____
_____
_____

Name_____

_____

_____

_____

_____

Name_____

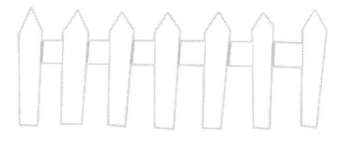

_____

_____

_____

_____

_____

_____

_____

_____

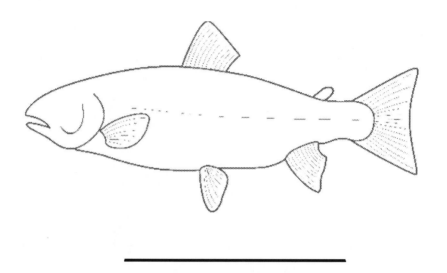

_____

_____

_____

_____

Name_____

_____

_____

_____

_____

Name_____

_____

_____

_____

_____

Name_____

_____

_____

_____

_____

Name_____

_____

_____

_____

_____

Name_____

_____

_____

_____

_____

Name_____

_____

_____

_____

_____

Name_____

_____

_____

_____

_____

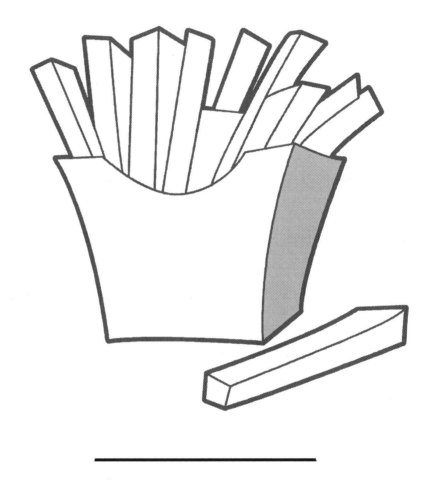

_____

_____

_____

_____

Name_____

_____

_____

_____

_____

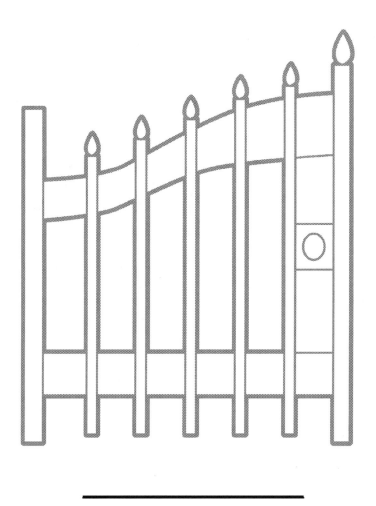

_____

_____

_____

_____

Name_____

_____

_____

_____

_____

_____

_____

_____

_____

Name_____

_____

_____

_____

_____

_____

_____

_____

_____

_____

Name_____

_____

_____

_____

_____

Name_____

_____

_____

_____

_____

Name_____

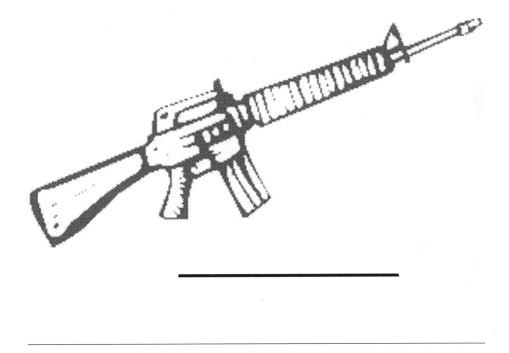

_____

_____

_____

_____

_____

_____

_____

_____

Name_____

_____

_____

_____

_____

Name_____

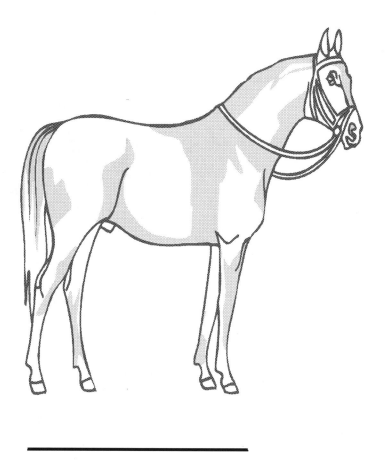

_____

_____
_____
_____

Name_____

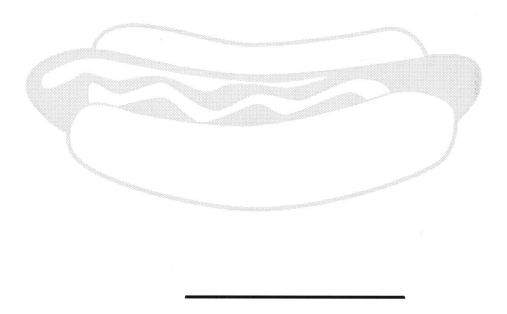

_____

_____

_____

_____

Name_____

_____

_____

_____

_____

Name_____

_____

_____

_____

_____

84

Name_____

_____
_____
_____
    .

Name_____

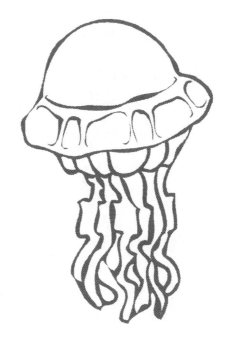

_____

_____

_____

_____

_____

_____
_____
_____

_____

_____

_____

_____

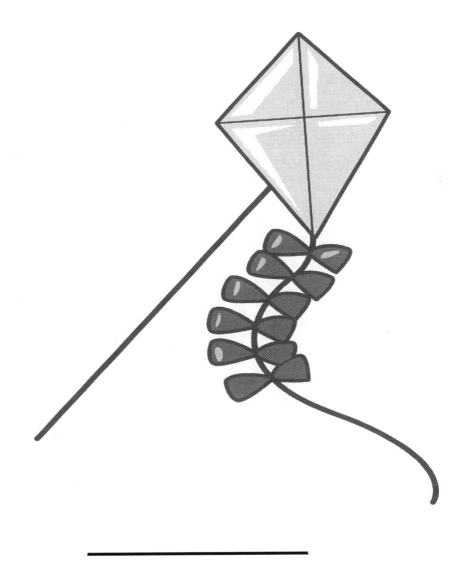

_____

_____

_____

_____

Name_____

_____

_____

_____

_____

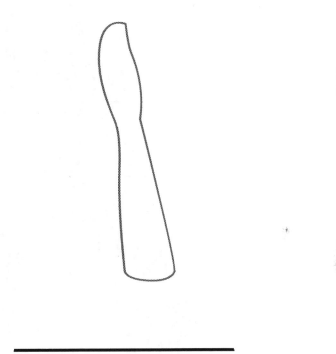

_____

_____

_____

_____

Name_____

—————————

_____

_____

_____

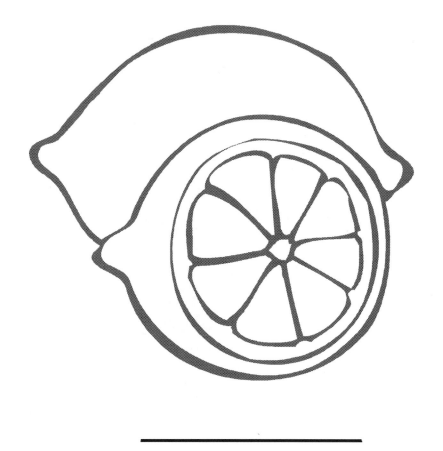

_____

_____
_____
_____

Name_____

_____

_____

_____

_____

Name_____

_____

_____
_____
_____

Name_____

_____

_____

_____

_____

Name

_____

_____

_____

_____

Name_____

_____

_____

_____

_____

Name_____

_____

_____

_____

_____

Name_____

_____

_____

_____

_____

_____

_____

_____

_____

Name_____

_____

_____

_____

_____

Name_____

_____

_____

_____

_____

Name_____

_____

_____

_____

_____

Name_____

_____

_____

_____

_____

Name_____

_____

_____

_____

_____

Name_____

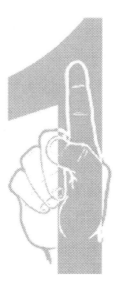

_____

_____

_____

_____

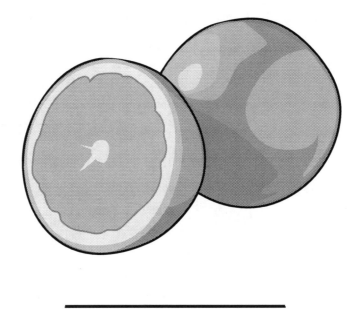

_____

_____

_____

_____

Name_____

_____

_____

_____

_____

Name_____

_____

_____

_____

_____

_____

_____

_____

_____

Name_____

_____

_____

_____

_____

_____

_____

_____

_____

Name_____

‾‾‾‾‾‾‾‾‾‾‾‾‾‾‾

_____

_____

_____

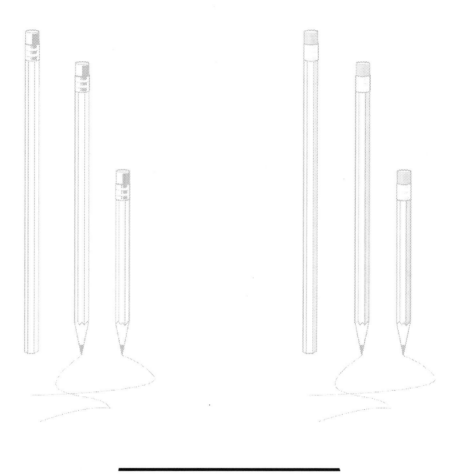

Name_____

———————————————

_____

_____

_____

Name_____

_____

_____

_____

_____

_____

_____

_____

_____

_____

_____
_____
_____

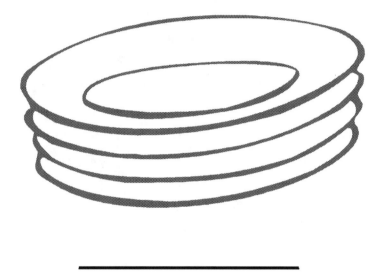

_____

_____

_____

_____

_____

_____

_____

_____

Name_____

_____

_____

_____

_____

Name_____

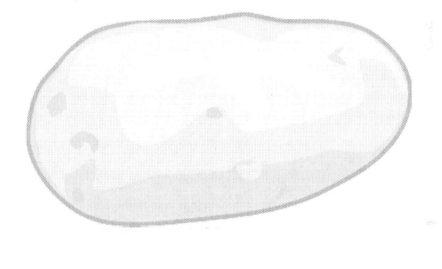

_____

_____

_____

_____

Name_____

_____

_____

_____

_____

Name_____

_____

_____

_____

_____

Name_____

_____

_____

_____

_____

Name_____

_____

_____

_____

_____

Name_____

_____

_____

_____

_____

Name_____

_____

_____
_____
_____

132

_____

_____
_____
_____

Name_____

━━━━━━━━━━━━

_____

_____

_____

Name_____

_____

_____

_____

_____

Name_____

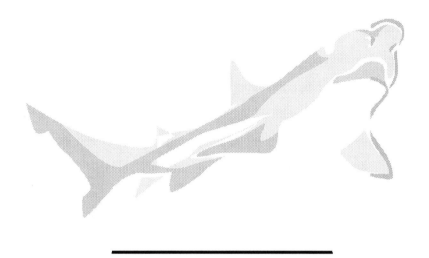

_____

_____

_____

_____

Name_____

_____

_____

_____

_____

Name_____

_____

_____

_____

_____

_____

_____

_____

_____

Name_____

_____

_____
_____
_____

Name_____

_____

_____

_____

_____

142

Name_____

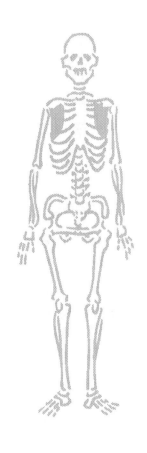

_____

_____
_____
_____

_____

_____

_____

_____

Name_____

_____

_____

_____

_____

_____

_____

_____

_____

Name_____

_____

_____

_____

_____

Name_____

_____

_____

_____

_____

Name_____

_____

_____
_____
_____

Name_____

_____

_____

_____

_____

Name_____

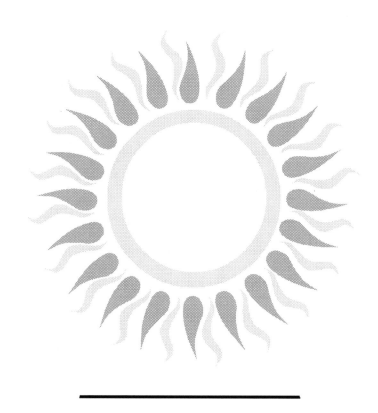

_____

_____

_____

_____

_____

_____

_____

_____

_____

_____

_____

_____

Name_____

_____

_____
_____
_____

156

Name_____

_____

_____

_____

_____

_____

_____

_____

_____

_____

Name_____

_____

_____
_____
_____

Name_____

_____

Name_____

_____

_____
_____
_____

Name_____

_____

_____

_____

_____

163

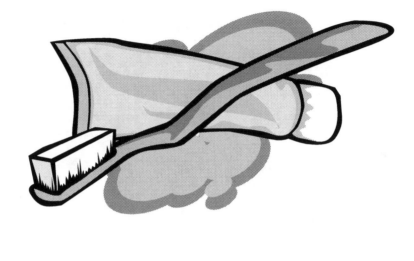

_____

_____

_____

_____

Name_____

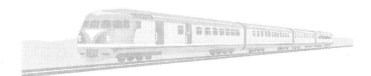

_____

_____

_____

_____

Name_____

_____

_____
_____
_____

Name_____

_____

_____

_____

_____

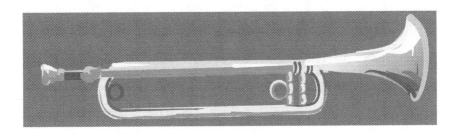

_____

_____

_____

_____

Name_____

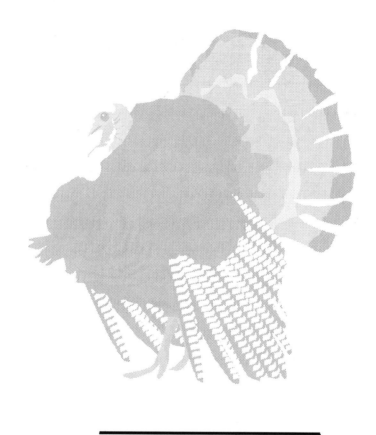

_____

_____

_____

_____

Name_____

_____

_____

_____

_____

_____

_____

_____

_____

_____

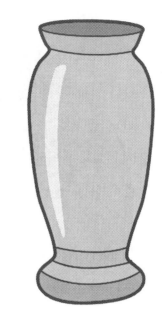

Name_____

_____

_____
_____
_____

_____

Name_____

_____

_____

_____

_____

Name_____

_____

_____

_____

_____

Name_____

_____

_____
_____
_____

_____

_____

_____

_____